Mountain Offerings

Praise for *Mountain Offerings*

"*Mountain Offerings* lovingly transports us from mountain to lake and back again, across sand-stippled memories, lingering in the heart's most intimate moments with a reverent awareness of their literal and figurative landscapes. Each poem is indeed a glorious offering of gratitude to and for the natural world and our experiences of it—and so, of each other."

—Jennine Capó Crucet, author of *Say Hello to My Little Friend*

"From the very first lucid lines of *Mountain Offerings* by Amy Allen, the collection of poems seems committed—through brevity and clarity and lean strength—to tell the truth of a life. There are elements that are ephemeral, from drip castles to wild onions to snow, and there are riddles, like overturned lifeboats, and a lost mother's found orchids. It feels like a promise from poet to the reader: she will not lie or put on a show. All of it is clear as water, burned to its essence, radiant with natural light."

—Jardine Libaire, author of *White Fur* and *Here Kitty Kitty*

"These narrative, fictive poems capture life, love and loss, the passage of time, longing, and what it means to live now, with an optimism and grace as clear as a Vermont stream. Highly recommended."

—Thomas Christopher Greene, author of *Notes from the Porch*

"Mountain Offerings delicately unfurls a sequence of emotional and ecological landscapes. Wild onions and fiddlehead ferns, flower 'imposters in the upturned soil'—Allen conjures a richly specific sense of place. In the backyard gardens, ocean docks, and mountain trails of this collection, nature emerges as the fulcrum between the past, the present, and the possible."

—Sonia Feldman, winner of the 2023 PEN/Robert J. Dau Short Story Prize for Emerging Writers

"Allen explores geography, emotions, and family in this collection. In the opening poem, the Vermont-based author luxuriates in nature, admiring birds while others attempt to photograph the sunset over Lake Champlain. A musical ode to the Green Mountain State inspires the speaker and her friends to dance and rejoice, 'united in the knowledge of the gift we call home.' ... A heartfelt and resonant collection of poetry."

—*Kirkus Reviews*

Mountain Offerings

poems by

Amy Allen

Montpelier, VT

Mountain Offerings copyright 2023 ©Amy Allen
All Rights Reserved.
Release Date: April 2, 2024

Printed in the USA.

Published by Rootstock Publishing
an imprint of Ziggy Media LLC
Montpelier, Vermont 05602
info@rootstockpublishing.com
www.rootstockpublishing.com

ISBN: 978-1-57869-190-6
Library of Congress Control Number: 2023921195
eBook ISBN: 978-1-57869-191-3

Cover art by Lindsey Taylor.
Book design by Eddie Vincent, ENC Graphics Services.

Author photo by Martin Wilson.

For permissions or to schedule a poetry reading or workshop, contact the author at www.allofthewritewords.com/contact.

For Martin, Lindsey & Griffin—my forever muses.

CONTENTS

Pilgrimage 1

An Anthem for the Green Mountain State 2

Foraging 3

Open Water 4

June's Promise: a Song of Innocence 6

January in Vermont 8

Krummholz 9

Tiny House 10

Emergence 11

My Mother's Flowers 12

Ascension 14

Gathering 16

Daughter of Mine 17

The Greenhouse 18

Brotherhood of the Brotherless 20

Freefall 21

Monitors 22

Apple Season 23

The Boys and Girls of Summer: a Song of Experience 24

Acknowledgments 25

About the Author 27

Pilgrimage

People arrive by car, on foot and on bikes.
Some bring dogs who chase frisbees
and each other out into the lake's shallows
oblivious to the show before them.
Some hold toddlers
who mimic the *oohs* and *aahs*
of adults surrounding them.

The lovers hold hands
their shoulders touching
heads tipped together.
The teens hold up their phones
adjusting settings in a hurried quest
to perfectly capture the glowing ball

as it eases down into Lake Champlain.
She prefers her spot alone in the woods
reclining on a flat rock
jacket balled under her head
surrounded by the pines and maples.
The only soundtrack from the birds
passing back and forth overhead
in a sort of rushed commute.

Their bellies are illuminated with golden light
the undersides of their wings aglow
with the sun's final offering.
She knows from the pinks and oranges
visible through the trees
the beauty that exists out on the horizon
but her pilgrimage is here, in the margins

with the quiet shade and the reverence
in knowing what can never be captured.

An Anthem for the Green Mountain State

an ode to Noah Kahan

In the Sixties, Dylan sang for an entire generation
in lyrics that unified and inspired
those who now lament
the emptiness of modern music.

And sixty years later a young man
from Strafford, Vermont, with a wide smile, a ponytail and a guitar
penned an album and a song that put us on the map
giving Vermonters—young and not so young—
an anthem.

He travels the country
steps up on stages and sings about our little state,
the fans cheering and belting out every single word
but we all know—that song is ours.

Somehow in its simple poetry able to capture
our landscapes worthy of painting
our connections to neighbors—
deep like the ruts in our dirt roads—
our creators and our thinkers and
our open-armed acceptors.

That summer we danced together
in grassy fields as the sky exploded from purple
to orange then pink over Champlain,
anticipating the sweet refrain—

"I LOVE VERMONT!" we screamed
feeling seen and heard
awash in the sky's brilliance
and in the majesty of our mountains
united in the knowledge of the gift we call home.

Foraging

I met you after school
where you told me you'd be waiting.
Your sweaty fingers encircled my wrist
pulling me through the thicket
and as I watched pink splotches arise on my bare legs
I envied your long pants.
But I would have followed you anywhere.

You were already busy digging
pulling out the wild onions
tossing them into a pile and laughing
when I asked if we could actually eat them.
You said I worried too much.

In the kitchen I filled a pot with water
as you washed our harvest
the white sink clouding brown as the dirt fell away.
I watched you work the big knife through them.
Your shoulder touched mine
as you dropped them in to boil.

After some stirring you poured off
the green tinged water and
dumped them into a bowl.
You put one on your fork
and stretched out your arm, holding my gaze.
The taste was sharp
and I couldn't wait for more.

Open Water

She met him downtown at a pet store
called Howl. His red vest
was oversized and the white name tag
pinned to it said Daisy.

He showed her where the fish bowls
were and gave detailed instructions
about how to safely transplant
her betta to its new home.

"Daisy's an interesting name,"
she commented, reaching for
the rubber plant outstretched in his palm.
"Oh, that's my dog," he explained.
"The manager told us to put
our pet's names on there to help
start conversations with customers."

At the register he said *yes*
when she asked him if he'd like
to hang out sometime. He handed her
a pen that was tied with twine
to a jar of treats so she could
write down her number.

Later, when he stood at her door
not in his uniform but wearing a Nirvana
t-shirt and black Converse high tops
she said, "Hey Daisy" and they smiled,
knowing that this would be their joke.

"Be sure to have her back by curfew!"
her mom yelled from her spot
deep in the couch cushions.
She rolled her eyes and reached

for his hand and she knew
that the night was hers
and it was theirs
and they turned toward the road
that glittered out before them.

June's Promise: a Song of Innocence

Upon arrival shoes were tossed hastily
deep into the back of the closet
clothes dumped into squeaky drawers
before bare feet would fly down the stairs
and the screen door smacked a goodbye.

Met with thick, salty air we hobbled
across the driveway of crushed shells
and pushed aside cobwebs to pump air
into deflated bike tires and we were free.

Days were spent on faded beach towels
and searching for blue sea glass
and for the perfect wave.
We made rope bracelets
and drip castles and took
wobbly tandem rides with friends.
We bought snow cones
from the ice-cream truck
which stained our tongues
and dripped down our wrists.

The deli guy gave us chicken livers
folded inside thick paper
tied neatly with twine.
We squealed as we tied the slick organs
to transparent string, dropping them down
into the dark water, standing by
with green nets ready to swoop
under the crabs' blueish-gray bodies.

Late afternoon we stepped into outdoor showers
using bars of soap housed in clamshell dishes
the embedded grains of sand
rough against sunburned skin.

The suds pooled around our ankles
and poured out into the driveway like sea foam.

And when we were finally released
from family dinner tables
it was back to the beach
for jumping off lifeguard stands
down into the cool sand
and for lying on our backs
to search the sky for something
that was bigger than we felt.

We thought we knew it all
and yet the one thing we missed
is all that we would be willing
to give one day just to be here again
with our calloused feet
and a season of endless possibility.

January in Vermont

Afternoons are fleeting, their daylight
quickly replaced by brilliant oranges
and pinks spreading and easing
down into Lake Champlain.

Soon a three-quarter moon takes stage,
a spotlight on snow-covered hills
illuminating the journey as our car slips
through woodstove smoke suspended

above the pavement, like a phantom tollbooth.
A solitary cow stands
just outside a lopsided dairy barn seeping
warm yellow light out into the night air.

Her saucer eyes are fixed out to where the sky
joins the lake. The stars always shine brightest
on the coldest of days,
a reward just for making it.

Krummholz

I like it up here
among these crooked trees
a bonsai paradise
everything gnarled and stunted
jutting at weird angles
the greens as dark as green gets.

You hand me a sprig of edelweiss
and I remember my mother
how she would give several turns
to the music box atop my dresser
as she tucked me in each night.

Resting for a moment beside me
she sang along as she leaned down
kissing my forehead as I breathed in
the sweet smell of her face cream.

After she shut the door behind her
I'd watch as the plastic ballerina spun around
in her gauzy skirt, the notes getting further
and further apart as she slowed to a stop.

I tuck the white flower into the base of my braid,
toe at a lichen-covered rock with my mud-caked boot
thinking how there's no one left now
to love me that way.

And yet there's you to lean against
resting atop this windswept mountain
unfurling yet intertwined, together here
among these twisted persistent trees.

Tiny House

Mud season, Vermont's weakest offering
the white cabin walls stark
against so much brown.

Drawers cleverly tucked
into stair treads, less quaint
when they jammed against their runners.

You flipped a switch and the fireplace
hummed orange. We played gin on the loveseat
and the cards slid between the cushions.

When we made love I drew
your damp forehead against mine, knuckles
grazing the ceiling, the bedding smelled of garlic.

In the morning, as you descended to join me
I noticed I could nearly reach
to pour you coffee from the toilet.

After the sunrise and omelets
it was clear we'd exhausted
the square footage. Perhaps to nourish

the desire for such close quarters,
the potential must exist
to stand up and walk away.

Emergence

She runs her fingertips
atop the shiny fiddleheads
tightly curled like a baby's fist
around its mother's pinky.

Next to them the daffodil greens
have shot up and will soon pop
with their yellow and white flowers
which always feel like relief.

Inhaling the evening air
thick with lilac she notes that
the daylight holds on just long enough
to offer hope. And the next morning

the fiddleheads have suddenly released,
unfurling their spirals
into elongated majestic ferns. It's as though
they are acting out her heart.

My Mother's Flowers

Florida feels like vacation
except when you're there to sort
through your dead mother's things.

We moved through her house
south end to north—
keep, donate, toss.

Heavy-lidded casserole dishes
cookbooks with margin notes
penciled in her cursive
framed photos of ourselves
leather handbags we'd given her on birthdays
three unopened jars of her face cream—
I wondered when I'd forget that smell.

After an evening dip in the backyard pool
that felt like cheating
my brother rolled the cans down the driveway
stacking the overflow into tidy towers.
I looped brown twine
around a stack of unread newspapers
the way my father used to
like securing a bakery box

and there in one of the cans
were my mother's flowers
the pots tipped on their sides.
They came tumbling out of their terra-cotta
sprawling yellow hibiscus with
surprising pink centers
purple bougainvillea
like miniature flowering trees
and slender white orchids, their tall
stems lovingly clipped to thin stakes

offering support for their heavy heads.
I worked on my knees in the dark
digging down past the mulch
making a shallow home for each and
casting their pots aside as I pressed
and leveled the earth around them.

In the morning as we pulled away from the house
I touched her ring on a chain
heavy like a thumb pressed against my chest
and remembered how after our visits
she would stand out front waving
long after we'd rounded the corner

Now the flowers gazed back at me
imposters in newly upturned soil.
I closed my eyes and prayed for rain.

Ascension

Arising from the green valley
where goats amble, munching grass
and sounding the bells around their necks
the glacier is revealed.

Snowy, jagged peaks
dare us to approach—
there is such disharmony
in its two seasons.

We scale its trails in
black fly heat
with shallow breaths that give
our stories offbeat punctuation.

Over the ridge we welcome
cooler air and you motion
to a sapphire lake—
a reward for the climb.

We are pulled to its edge
and without discussion
we peel off sweaty socks
and plunge our feet in.

Slick brown tadpoles dart
across our submerged flesh.
Their squat, newly sprouted
legs out of place on their squirming bodies.

Like teenagers they swim around suspended
caught in a world between
first loves and still falling asleep
next to childhood stuffed toys each night.

Our backs recline against
sun-baked rocks and I know
that someday I will wish
to be back in this moment.

Without ever touching you
I am holding your hand
I am kissing your forehead
looking inside you and
deciding to stay here.

You thought you knew mountains—
And then
this.

Gathering

You held out your palm
and asked me if I knew that pinecones

opened in the heat, each scale unfurling
to release their seeds.

My fingers traced the ridges
as you spoke.

Our daughter was busy collecting them
making little piles

underneath the swing set
before begging you for a push.

She shrieked and laughed
as you lifted her higher

than I ever would have dared
and I winced when I heard them

crunch under your boots
but she'd already forgotten her treasure.

Later that night I smiled to see
you'd left one on my bedside table

a fugitive from the yard
one perfectly spiraled survivor.

I lifted the covers and slid in beside you
my chilled limbs seeking yours.

Daughter of Mine

Your evenly tanned limbs
are tossed carelessly over the couch
as your head tips back with a smile so broad
and a laugh suggesting you've seen
far more than possible in your fifteen years.

Thick, dark lashes curled perfectly upwards
accentuated by a practiced eye roll
that I know as your signature move.
You are a girl
in the figure of a woman.

You still belt out songs from *Annie*
in the shower when you think we aren't listening
and it must feel like life is full of hard knocks
when you are a girl who is desperate to leave
yet still wants to be tucked in each night.

I am awed as I watch you move
through your world, armed with a resolve
I still do not possess. And somehow reconciling
these versions of you is as complex
and tormenting as learning how to love myself.

The Greenhouse

On a corner lot
nestled among two-story homes
wooden swing sets
and paved driveways
stands a glass greenhouse.

Black framing lines
each window and door,
and a warm light reveals
leafy vines and rows of plants
spread out over wooden tables.

On eight winter mornings
I escaped there
running through the cold
while my daughter lay
under fluorescent lights
and heated blankets,
working on not dying.

Most days a woman was inside
her arms raised as she tended
the hanging plants
or hunched forward when she worked
on the rows of terra-cotta pots.

I watched her train vines
up a mesh screen.
I watched as she tipped
a copper can over each plant
gently moistening the soil.

On eight winter mornings
I paused there, resting
my hands on my thighs

as I caught my breath
before the inevitable return.

On eight winter mornings
I left my daughter's room
moved past patients slumped in wheelchairs
and visitors with nervous half smiles.

Outside, I'd pull the cool air
into my lungs, my sneakers
crunching on salted pavement.
I'd turn to spot my daughter's window
guilty for the relief I felt in leaving.

On eight winter mornings
I'd run until I felt the fear
turn to a dull ache
that moved through my limbs.
I willed myself to feel
the humidity—an embrace
that existed within those glass walls.

On eight winter mornings
the greenhouse saved me
while the doctors saved my child.
And leaving the hospital
felt as much a gift
as the woman who made the choice
to cultivate life right there in the midst
of so much cold.

Brotherhood of the Brotherless

There's a bittersweet kinship
among those who've lost a sibling

a strange comfort in all
that does not need to be spoken.

Like how it feels to take a seat
at the Thanksgiving table

or to line up for family pictures
at weddings and graduations

knowing there should be another chair
at the table, another body

to drape your arm around in the photo.
There should be an asterisk

on everything that comes after.
And while we all just keep getting grayer

and more tired and freckled and wrinkled
our brothers remain captured, suspended

in yellowed 3x5 photographs with curved edges
stuck in thick, chestnut-haired days

wearing their faded, ripped cutoffs
their tanned, toned limbs gleaming

and wide grins spread effortlessly
across their faces in anticipation

for all that is surely to come.

Freefall

They have been on the trail
for nearly two hours yet
she doesn't even notice
her hunger until they pause.

She makes a tabletop out of a flat rock
and sits, wiping her forehead
watching as he pulls a bag of snacks
and a pocket knife from his pack.

The blade slides through
the green apple's skin
pulling slices from the core.
He holds every other one out to her.

A nod of his head means it's time
to pack up and return to their ascent
and they settle back into a rhythm
of footfalls and pushing branches aside.

Light begins to land differently
signaling the top and they soon emerge.
She sips her water while he points
identifying peaks in the distance.

Her boot toes at a small rock
and it cartwheels off the edge. She tracks it
as it bounces against boulders
until it's finally out of sight.

Her breath catches as she considers
how with just one choice
she could be that rock
charting her own way down
reckless and unencumbered.

Monitors

There's an implied understanding
in the family lounge
at the children's hospital
that we will discuss
the persistent light rainfall
or the questionable sushi
from the deli downstairs.

Making conversation like actors
in an extended improv where we play people
who bumped into one another
on the stained couches
of a car service lounge
or shifting in metal folding chairs
in the back of a sticky school gymnasium
awaiting the orchestra concert's first note.

Our stiff limbs reveal the toll
of nights spent curled into vinyl chairs
eyes alert at every beep
watching intently for the rise
and fall of chests under blankets.

Our hearts can't bear to feel anything
for fear of feeling everything
so we smile meekly
lament the weak coffee
and resume our synchronous
solitary vigils.

Apple Season

As August days grow shorter
the apples begin to fall
the weight of the fruit too much
for knobby branches to bear.

Each drops with a thud
the ones we don't gather
soon smashed into the grass
by the lawn tractor.

Smeared fruit attracts honey bees
who hover over the flesh
and we remind ourselves
not to walk barefoot.

Neighbors come by to fill
bags and bags, holding up their toddlers
to reach high branches
the way we used to with our own children

who would help us rinse and peel
standing on footstools at the counter
learning how to pinch the dough
and the house would smell full.

Now long gone living in houses
with kitchens and children of their own
though we still refer to their empty
bedrooms here using their names.

Today you surprised me in the kitchen
a bundle of apples gathered in the lower half
of your outstretched t-shirt. I reached for the flour
pulled out the peelers, and we fell into rhythm.

The Boys and Girls of Summer: a Song of Experience

Our calloused bare feet pushed
against ridged bike pedals each evening
making our way to the beach at twilight.

Sitting in a small circle we'd rest
wine coolers on our tanned bare knees
and play truth or dare
as the sun slipped into the bay.

We sang along to Joni Mitchell and
the Indigo Girls strummed on the guitar
eventually pairing off as the darkness
of nightfall emboldened us.

Your fingers interlaced mine as we walked
up to the overturned lifeboat near the dunes.
We worked together pushing the cool sand
aside so we could slide underneath where it was quiet.

All we had to worry about was making curfew
and the way it felt to lean into each other
accompanied by the soundtrack
of the waves arriving and retreating

and of our friends' laughter
there under the shimmering moonlight
that danced across the ocean's surface
comforted by the knowledge that tomorrow
we'd get to do it all over again.

Acknowledgments

Thank you to the literary journals who accepted and published several of these poems, giving me the confidence to continue my writing journey:

"Ascension" *Atlanta Review,* November 1, 2021

"Brotherhood of the Brotherless"
The Write Launch Literary Magazine, June 1, 2023

"Foraging"
Poetry Society of Vermont, *The Mountain Troubadour,* May 1, 2023

"Gathering" *West Trade Review,* June 18, 2023

"January in Vermont" *The Moving Force Journal,* October 28, 2022

"Krummholz" *Fauxmoir Lit Mag,* April 5, 2022

"Monitors" *Months to Years,* August 31, 2021

"My Mother's Flowers"
Sunflowers at Midnight Magazine, May 11, 2022

"Open Water" *The Write Launch Literary Magazine,* June 1, 2023

"The Greenhouse"
The Write Launch Literary Magazine, June 1, 2023

"Tiny House" *Pine Row Press,* April 1, 2021

Thank you to my publisher, Samantha Kolber, and the team at Rootstock Publishing for taking on this project and for believing in me. How rewarding to work with a Vermont-based company!

Thank you to my husband for his genuine belief that I have something valuable to say, and for supporting my craft by letting me read my work aloud to him and by holding down the fort when I'm off at writer's conferences, even the ones held in beautiful Sicily!

Thank you to my children for showing me the true meaning of love, and for their excitement (even if slightly feigned!) at the news of each poem publication over the years, and at the publication of this chapbook.

Thank you to my family and friends for being my biggest cheerleaders; to Sandra Khalil for her thoughtful editing and friendship; to my college professors, namely Barry Goldensohn, Steven Millhauser, Kathryn Davis, and Victor Cahn, for teaching me the craft of writing both in the classroom and via their own work; to Jardine Libaire–a beacon of creativity and talent for me from the 1990s through the present; and to Jane Cole for inspiring me to both study and teach English, and to hold myself to the highest possible standards, in all facets of life.

Finally, thank you to my parents, without whom I would most certainly not be here, both literally and figuratively. I miss them every day.

Amy Allen (she/her) studied English literature and creative writing at Skidmore College and at Drew University. Her poetry has been published in a variety of journals, including *West Trade Review*, *The Write Launch*, *The Mountain Troubadour*, *Pine Row Press*, *Months to Years*, *Atlanta Review*, *Fauxmoir Lit Mag*, *The Moving Force Journal*, and *Sunflowers at Midnight*. She lives in Shelburne, Vermont with her husband, children, and dogs, and is blessed to enjoy time outdoors in the beautiful Green Mountain State throughout all seasons of the year. She owns All of the Write Words, a freelance writing/editing business, a profession that thankfully allows her the time to write for pleasure.

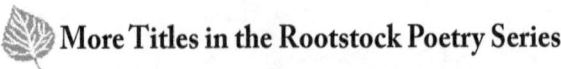 **More Titles in the Rootstock Poetry Series**

Fire on a Circle by Kim Ward

Indigo Hours: Healing Haiku by Nancy Stone

Lifting Stones by Doug Stanfield

PoemCity Anthology 2023 by Kellogg-Hubbard Library

PoemCity Anthology 2024 by Kellogg-Hubbard Library

Safe as Lightning by Scudder H. Parker

Stonechat by Mary Elder Jacobsen

The Lost Grip by Eva Zimet

To the Man in the Red Suit by Christina Fulton

Unleashed: Poems & Drawings by Betty Nadine Thomas

Poetry submissions are open. Learn more and submit at www.rootstockpublishing.com.

Printed in the USA
CPSIA information can be obtained
at www.ICGtesting.com
CBHW032002090924
14064CB00006B/40